HOW TO identify a predator or prey?

HOW TO identify a predator or prey?

by
Grace E Espiritusanto

HOW TO identify a predator or prey?

Author: Grace E Espiritusanto

Published September 2021

Published in the United States
printing number
1 2021 First Edition

Book Catalog Information:

Espiritusanto, Grace E

HOW TO identify a predator or prey? /Grace E Espiritusanto –1st Ed

p. .cm
Including bibliographical references(p.) and index
ISBN-13 978-0-578-98720-0
ISBN-10 0-578-98720-1
1.predator 2. prey 3. abuser 4. scammers I Title

Where to Send All Inquiries
All inquiries regarding this book may be sent by email to the attention of Grace E Espiritusanto, graceeespiritusanto1@gmail.com

C

To people that want what you have. or to be you , everything that you do is important maybe you saying why? People want to be you! You're not a celebrity or somebody important. I'm thinking the same thing but in this book, you're going to know what I'm talking about and then you tell me if I'm not prey or what? everything that I do is important. what is a prey? a creature or a person that is hunted and killed for food by another animal or person. What does predator mean?

Opportunistic predators can be defined as those whose attack on prey is conditioned by the spatial and temporal co-occurrence of both as well as by certain environment or physiological conditions that trigger the person that Is hunted and killed for food by another or a person. trigger the use of alternatives preys for survival.I'm writing all these definitions to give you a clear understanding of my story, I'm prey to these individuals so I did a search. and got all the definitions they trigger woman that been divorced single woman young and old specially after a loss or a depression vulnerable you are an easy target for them you need someone next to you, in other words, you feel weak.

May be you are saying to yourself why she's talking about this? because my whole life since I was 10 years old and then 13 years old I been hunted for loving someone like loving a person is a sin that wasn't the problem is that they keep messing with me this guy was his ex even though I keep saying I don't want to be bothered with that till this day is hunting me down.so I'm entitled to tell my story and till now he doesn't stop. you are probably saying to yourself she's exaggerating when you start reading you could also be a pray to a person and you don't even know it, I'm not and that's why I'm going into details fig he was someone that knew me before I knew him.

Listen I apply for jobs and as soon I apply they be like this job is not available, no we going to proceed with another person and I have the qualifications this person in power wants to stop me from everything that I want to do in my life and for everything they find a justification this man hates me that's why my story needs to be heard. he was with him so all he's ex come after me ex woman and man now that

I'm putting two and two together is that I could remember things that he did to me from the beginning he's intentions of getting close to me were never to love me.

it was a setup he hates me because of this man and I guess he needed to keep me closed to him that's a psychopath mentality is like killing you slowly charming at the beginning they tell you always what you want to hear they don't have no morals or principles unresponsive of feeling and emotions they see you as a quick win, let me give you an example of what im talking about on December 03,2019 my daughter graduating ceremony so i'm getting ready the ceremony starts at 4:30pm so like about 3:30pm I get a call from social security this man gives me his name badge number and I listen to what he had to say he's saying that I have 21 accounts with thousands of dollars on my name even internationally involved in money laundry and in drugs so what they need to do is freeze my account and me to go social security and take my money to one agent that was going to wait for me there and they was going to give me a new social security card I was like listen that's not me I only have a join account with my children he ask me how much I had in my account I told him I only $3000 at this moment why you don't freeze that mans account and leave people alone I went and withdrawal my money in the bank Im like is 4pm they closed social security at five this is a scheme but is always in the time that you have an event going on to distract you.

I hang up the phone and went to my daughter's graduation the other sister count go because she in school upstate New York the other sister was taking a test her finals she graduates in may her best friend was there and they call her and me together banner of honors my daughter in front of everyone and they took pictures of us she graduated with honors I'm so proud of her so we had like a nice dinner it was a buffet of pasta chicken parmigiana, pasta alfredo, grilled salmon garlic bread, and cookies cake chocolate pudding a nice variety of stuff my daughter Patricia had a little bit of everything I gave salmon to josh he eat a little bit of what I was eating he wanted to run around and play in front of the audience instead of course so after we eat I left the ceremony has past when dinner came they were talking josh kept running around a lot and I knew pat was going to go out with her friend and she did. So I was prey before my daughter's graduation. Think about it, you are rushing to see your daughter and they are trying to stop you from doing what you want to do.

The symptoms of a predator? They are watching you constantly they talk to you normally and sometimes they have kids your kid's ages with this kid they want to set up your kids hanging out with them and getting them into bad things like shoplifting doing things they not suppose to be doing pear preacher bad crowd could get you into bad habits if you are young, inexperienced hard to identify them because you are prey and they say what you want to hear, sometimes is your personality that attracts them is not your fault these people are sick mentally and emotionally and if they rich or they with people with power is worse because they could mess up your life up so much as they did with me .they also have clones till the next chapter of life.

These are questions to ask yourself? When I became a target, how old I was when this happened? Why me, to be honest, I still don't know why these people are maniacs is like he sends this person after me his lover Mr Adonis! man and woman I don't understand why or yes to obtain his objective this woman leaves her door open every time i'm going down to see if I say something about her or she comes out at the same time in several occasions I heard her on the phone and she was saying if she coming down now so she has someone that inform her if I'm going up or down this is the woman that has an order of protection against me and shes chasing me around I been very careful because is obvious what is the purpose of this they gave her a 2years order of protection so she feels that a year past so she needs to get me arrested before her order of protection expired 12/2020 everything is calculated

He writes it in his song this man likes to arrest people that's the way he can obtain your personal belongings is a group of Crookes that work together doing witchcraft to you he has a person in every floor doing all type of witchcraft also throws powder In the floors so you could step on them,while you going up the steps, is a constant harassment as soon as I walk in my floor he has this two woman from slamming her doors is 1:30am in the morning I heard them slamming the door at this time I got in at 1:00am because the train has a delay is days that I work 4pm to 12am Im putting my son in bed and getting everything ready for the morning because he's going to school and I have a sonogram appointment in the morning is time to removed my IUD im telling you my day to day agenda so you could have an understanding about why im saying Im a prey

They have problems so when they get rejected they become another person to get acceptances where you find a psychopath?1 at church yes don't get surprise 2- in the park as simple as taking your kids or your dog to the park 3-when you take your kids to school 4- it could also be a neighbor 5-when you get tons of coincidences happening to you 6-in a club or in a bar that you are a regular in a normal place like the laundry mat. Supermarket these people are watching you constantly, in other words, they could be in the least expected places.and you are not aware of it.sometimes you have to be very careful where you go and what you say to people and is hard when you a friendly person like me is people that constantly trying to get your info from asking you so much personal stuff apparently seems insignificant, is to know more about you from simple things to important things it may sound exaggerated but they could be hired to become your friend and I ask myself why I'm not even rich is simply evil I had to ask myself tons of questions but I still don't have an answer to me their motor is not strong enough for all of this.

What can you do to stop these people who you can contact don't stay quiet if you have to write in the newspapers, in social media if you are a student.talk to someone in school, do what I'm doing, write a book about they have the most simple excuses to hunt you down. If you date them and break up they hate you for that they can't take rejection and they don't know how to leave you alone is an excuse of a psychopath he's only purpose is to use you everything else is a lie.they always looking for an excuse the option of stopping and moved on don't exist in his calendar or his vocabulary at least until he obtains what he wants from you, in my case all my stuff like you don't have a say I don't believe people that with their mouth they say one thing and do another action talk louder than words how I know I'm a prey because they feel I'm a threat without saying or doing anything don't want to be with anyone the same thing happened on my birthday before I hang out with my kids another incident happened I could go on and on with you of all the things that been happening to me,

I don't call anybody this past year I been writing my books this is my second book of the things that were happening to me the reason i'm writing because I want to help others to come out of this situation and myself going back they like to observe what you like in all the aspects the colors the textures, your style even in man bold curly hair cute tall whatever is your preferences smart well dressed strong with muscle etc. The list goes on the salon you go too, you notice that they have a tendency of asking you questions and since you are relaxing you get a little open and talk things you not supposed to especially if you are married or doing something illegal you could be recorded and they save it for later when they need you and you not even aware of now I'm putting you on blast.he wanted to make people believe that I'm crazy and a very bad woman but everything that I'm saying is true he's a psychopath they get obsessed to destroyed you nothing obsessive is good in every sense of the word he knew I was going to write a book this is non- fiction this been my whole life and don't think because I'm writing this stopping no all this man wanted and wants to get my property is insane all the things that he's doing but when god is in your favor he turns bad thing for good to his believer God wants people to believe in him.going back to the story people think is a joke is not this man is a predator and he does this because he knows I'm never going to sleep with him.

One and two he had my ex as a side he wants to become me my essence is like this guy blames me if my ex left them. how many times he left me I'm not with the guy they find me as an obstacle loving a person is respecting his decisions you can't be by any circumstances violate people's rights why I'm writing this because everything, is connected he been sending people after me, for a long time why I wrote this title because all this stuff happened to me just for falling in love with this man as such a young age. Why this is a great book to read will help you identify a psychopath and the most important thing don't become what they want. be yourself is ironic but praying helps keep your mind healthy. Who should be my audience? adults and young adults is funny how money changes the scenarios you have money or power is ok you are poor without government influence they put you in jail they don't give you one chance this people rape do all type of crimes and is like they get away with it and sometimes you looking for a black person and he could be blond or vice versa or his clone could be your raise you understand? What I'm trying to say is that sometimes we are quick to judge people. with money you could become another raise just to hurt others and in their house they living a normal life with their family you understand the level of criminology sometimes we think is this one it could be the least expected person because they living double lives

Look at my situation this man is trying to hunt me down in public.for instance, They taking from my paid check 200 extra of taxes every time I get paid that's ten thousand four hundred dollars and this been happening for two years so my last year refund never got it $6,800 if add everything together $27,800 in this past two years this is an abuse of power when I have two dependents that I have to support them. So you understand I'm a pray! to this person in power and he still trying to set me up till this day the law should be for everybody human beings have right of who they want to be with nobody has the power to stop you from your life the way you want to this is controlling mentality and manipulating

I would never want to be with someone that I'm forcing love doesn't grow that's sick is so obvious because all he wants is to destroy my life is all of them gather for me, im their common denominator I know his tactic he gets all these cars and this person in the building outside to get me agitated so I could get nervous or panic every day I ask God for strength because at the beginning I gain some weight because i was anxious I'm innocent I don't know what's going on and I got scared this Findingo guy some looser that looking at all the characteristics I figured out that he's a psychopath that all he wanted was exploits me that's his purpose since day one.

This man never gave me anything instead I lost money been with him he registers a car under my name and then dumps it in the Bronx and the car gets full of tickets so I get a summons from the court when I went to court they tell me I owe $2,000 worth of tickets I had to paid that because he put that on my name and before that one day I told him that I wanted to come to Manhattan and in the highway we get into an accident and the car gets all mess up also the other person car was worse the insurance went up and they even got me in a lawsuit the insurance paid some money but a lawyer send a letter of a million dollars I don't know what settlement the insurance company had with the other party.so you understand this was from the beginning this is just one incident but it was several stuff that he did from the start his theory I hate you but I have you as a side because I hate you. And in everything all he did was use me.

Changing the topic this guy has a tendency of sending people to tell me what he did, or what his doing to mess me over, for instance, a person talking about the same situation I'm going throw find a way to tell me what they do throw another person this man is very evil. Like for instance I go to the motor vehicle and take all my proper identification and they miss spell my last name how if everything says my name he is pitty so I'm watching porn in my computer this man has a video describing how he wants my property and his going to take it and gives a detail explanation of what he wants to do.he sends people on the train doing all types of signs and all this conversation talking about stuff related to me.and people on bikes with target bags, with trees, guys with super t-shirts he just don't know how to stop he had put my own children against me.

Then mess with their stuff too like my little daughter they took $50dollars out of her account and my first daughter they were telling her she cant graduate from college because the stupid, was that had me as a side you believe that some messing lie.and my daughter Patricia they have her paying some cash she doesn't owe in an apartment she doesn't have a lease.is an abuse of power in all the sense of the word even in music videos like Nicky minah stupid hoe, he describes how much he hates me.

Look at my first marriage, it was in church martin Santana he gathers two names of different people and married me under that name he lie in the church he doesn't have any limits, so you understand why I'm saying you could be hunted in church.this made believe marriage lasted two years and a short time after he dies.conveniently so he doesn't have to pay child support because he didn't even had an active social security card and shortly after he moves in hes start receiving this mail with another name so I ask why you have mail of Rafael Bautista when your saying your name is martin, a cristian man he tells me that he's using this name of a dead man and he had a construction company under that dead man name, cash checks and everything

Even an id you understand so you understand now they follow me wherever I go or move when I got married I was only 23 years old he got me to marry him you believe how far this person could go scam people in church saying that he was selling apartment they gave him part of the money in total in church he scam, 10 different people, $70,000even the pastor was looking for him.he had a sob story that before me his wife die and his raising two sons by himself.he's the same person then Adonis knows martin and his sons what a coincidence he tells me he does make a lot scams a year later

They are the same person his seen uncover I understand he send a guys that he screws to rent my apartment they coming to leave in my building he's really after me he uses all this neighbors everyone i'm his target look at this ups guy this man tells me that he is with the person that had me as a side I don't know the man and he hate me too he's adding in the list all this new people that I don't even know about Im dealing with a psychopath he gather people that one time I went on a date and we didn't have chemistry how he knows who they are because he send them to me all for his plan.

Or people that they want to talk to you and you don't like them so now they also hate. also always comparing me to the worst never people that are doing good the mess ups. Sometimes I just laugh you would never be a man that I would want to sleep within this country we still have freedom of speech, I also had secret enemies the ones that laugh at your jokes and talk about you behind your back hate on the low but they pretend that you guys at least that's what you think they your friends and you are trusting this person he's a transporter of information this man writes songs expressing how much he hates people and even saying that you are sending people after me constantly trying to set me up blackmail me and many other things I'm telling you later on, how I survived don't trust anybody family friend husband boyfriend kids is sad but you need to save yourself.

Be very observant if you can ask for prayers of different people god will guide you, obstacles like if I wanted to stop my kid from getting their degree you should be happy that a person been with you or not they did well if you feel happy frustrating my goals and destroying my life you need to go get help at a mental hospital asap. visit a psychologist take Prozac, loof pills get mental health a doctor needs to help, You need to be happy that people you used to sleep with are better why you think god didn't give Satan a second chance he's a fair God but he knew that the devil wasn't going to change and he damage big group angels the fact that you want to damage others so he got thrown out of heaven when you wrong is ok but when your intentions are to damage massive people you got Satan mentality he knew that he will never repent his the only one that knows what's on your heart so moving forward last year I said to myself since I'm working here in time square I'm going to the consulate that is in 1501 43street a week later the place looks abandoned that Dominican consulate been there for many years.

Not no longer little things like this is what I'm talking about so Torro was a man that when we came from the Dominican republic we rented a room his building is also abandoned is things that apparently don't mean anything but it does at the same time this maniac mentality always after if you look at my life everything has to be according to his plans please tell me your feedback of what you think about my story i'm a pray or not in your understanding

I was going crazy at the beginning I ask myself why all this weird stuff keep happening to me, i'm going to write every college I work and my duties at does colleges, citi college my duty was access control, in hunter college, I was in the main building on 68 street and in Rosenvelt house at 65 street between third ave and park avenue,thats a mansion that was donated for the school they mostly do events and have a few classes that also have two penthouse apartment that they let professor that are teaching stay there if they live in another state.another school york college

I was working in the daycare and in the bookstore of the school.in Bmcc I was working in Barnes and nobles in the book store, in Hostos, I was in the parking area checking cars.I work here in the federal building for overtime everything has to be according to his predictions if I'm alive today is because it is a god in heaven this man been planning to destroy my life he been hard on this. is people that talk to you and laugh or even joke and that's the aggressor and you don't know it. What level of hate this man has for somebody that did me wrong? that's the craziest part of the story he acting like I murder somebody that's the level of hate and I'm not a murder so you got the wrong person.

In constant harassment, 24/7, I'm going to tell the copy in what we are different I learn from my mistakes and you continue doing them over and over.sometimes you need a person that loves you less and consider you more a person that considers you don't do all this, that's why I know that all this is bullshit look the difference between me and this person I'm never thirsty I'm not settling for less he has a complot of people what is a complot? A complot is a group of people that gather for the same purpose the main focus is to obtain his goal, and this is the reason I'm writing all these articles and adding it on this book.

So now I'm going tell some of there traits a constellation of a trait that comprises effective features interpersonal as well as impulsive and antisocial behavior the affective features include lack of guilt empathy, superficial charm dishonesty, manipulative, reckless risk-taking physical aggression they never recognized the rights of others they are covertly hostile domineering, seeing their victims as merely an instrument to be used.they may dominate and humiliate their victim's grandiose sense of self feels entitled to certain things as their rights. pathological lying is almost impossible for them to be truthful on a consistent basis can create and get caught up in a complex belief about their own power and abilities Extremely convincing and even able to pass lie detectors test no remorse shame or guilt a deep-seated rage is split off and repressed, is at their core.

They do not see others around them as people but only as they good sizing you upon first meeting psychopath will then quickly exploit any weakness or vulnerability they've found they have a laser-like ability to identify a person soft spot capitalizing on another big heart or willingness to fall for a tall scheme a quick win, a big score.in a personal relationship, a psychopath will gather all types of information about you only to use it against you later. antisocial personality and sociopath, they share a disregard for the rights of others, this disregard can surface through various behavior, blatantly ignoring one's own or others' safety lying or manipulating being irresponsible, frequently fighting or assaulting others and a lack of remorse for one behavior. diagnosed with an antisocial personality disorder, this is my research about this psychopath what they able to do? Can they get a cure no they will never be able to change? He's marry the woman that had a kid with that guy when I was a kid he doesn't have anything more then bringing people to the equation this man/woman can't stop messing with me and for no reason.

Now that I know that his with that guy I don't want him at all even if he begs me to listen stay with each other, so for instants, they got this man my brother in-law fired what a coincident now that he been working for me he got fired and the excuse was lame so he makes them do all this stuff and at the end mess them over and now adding two by two fig had a wife name marry that's the sniffer is that his marry. this man is sick.so now he's saying because we had sex when I was 20year old now I have to pay him you believe that. Listen to everything it was base on his grudge for the other guy so why the kiss has to be after me because the sniffer sends them. He's money-hungry to the extreme first mess up your life and they want your finance cash house even clothing is not a joke and his real purpose to get with me one is because of him and two when I was a little girl I accused him of burning the building he's burning side so he was Richard finding all I want to do is moved to another direction in my life, I don't want to be bothered with this people are toxic so the message here is if I had you had as a side they have to mess you over that's there a way of demonstrating their feelings towards you.

All a setup psychopath mentality they could low your self-esteem when I was done with that psycho fig even though I had tons of stitches when I had my second daughter I thought I had a problem in my vagina so I had a friend at the moment that when she's gave birth she had some tearing inside out and she was searching for a gym doctor specialized in the closing vagina so I told her I want to go with you we both went paid our consultation and doctor examines the both of us she got treat it for her thing but me he didn't find anything he asks me you had some much stitches I said yes your fine in there and he shows me how to do some vagina exercise but I always vibrate in my vagina after an orgasm he told me what to do and I was confident the doctor was like you don't even look like you gave birth to two children is that they gave me so many stitches with the both of then I'm sharing this just to let you know what this psychopath could do mentally to a woman.

C

This maniac he is saying this nasty and ghetto man-made a clone of bright in his mind he thought I was going to be with his clone that's not a real person is people without a soul that's really cold, listen just knowing who bright is fig is sad and the sniffer when I say the sniffer is because fig used to sniff coke all I want to do throw up you are the nasty person in the world for me I think after all of this I'm going to therapy that's how bad I feel you have to pay me for all the damages physically and mentally finding out who had me as a side cause me psychological problems is very hard for me to trust people one thing I don't understand about them how they buy clones and they don't even have basic thing to survive they don't have jobs or home nothing, is because with this clones is to obtain their purpose.you under what type of psychopath this people are? you probably think your married and have some children and it could be an old lady lock inside her house living two lives if are married to a clone that's not a real person you was like I was living a lie the only thing if you are prospering is not convenient for them for you to fingered out not just yet they want to see what could they get away with it, without you knowing they always the victim , I need to tell you the truth make sure your not in one of this categories that i'm describing this people are very sick and that's how they get you love is not an option don't get fool they incapable of feelings. moving forward, today I had a lock on my other room that I have the key in the key chain of all my padlocks, I go to the gym and lock my stuff and I don't have the key and looking at the patlock that wasn't mine so I recently change my locks and they have the key to my house how they get the key my brother in-law made a drama about he cant open my door I lost a day of work and he came with a lock man with two different lock now i know this is a setup they made copies of the keys before he brought the locks and they made me believe they was brand new but is ok i'm going to put some new locks and paid a new person and im not paid him even dough i said im not paying him i did i'm not doing what they want me to do so you understand how much this people mess with me. I had to sign some paper at the gym so the guy could clip my locker at the gym. a millionaire and his hype to get my apartment changing the subject if you had me as a side to cock block me it doesnt matter what counts is what you doing so I decide to go to the movies to distract myself a little I went to see black Christmas it was good it talk about ocultism that people think it doesnt exist but it does been for ages we have a tendency of things that we dont know we thing they not there bad people use all the resource to mess with you

All my life I been busting my ass for my children so they could have a decent life I didnt get no help till this day so now someone that been doing whatever with whoever they wants comes thinking hes going to get something from me you got to be out of your mind look at my son birthday past Christmas came he didnt get anything my daughter ceremony came she didnt get anything you understand how can you expect to get without giving so when the grapes where soured you didnt want some i mean that when I had to pay for all the kids stuff you didnt want to be part of that but now they getting sweet how can you grow a plant without the proper care you need to water it put in the son in life you have to help show mercy the same way you want people that have mercy on you my problem is to finish this book and continue writing to put out there all the things that happened to me. So to all his side I'm their common denominator so going back he makes all this theory to hide the real factor, such a psychopath

You don't have a say on this in their mentality they savage for money if you own something you are the main focus he doesn't have a preference or no he does he likes man but he fucks woman to get things fig told me he fucks woman but when he goes crazy is when a man puts him in doggie style.it makes sense send all his man lover go after me look at this I said that I'm studying and I been taking this practice prof quiz online to get me ready for the insurance because I want to take this test now January so today I'm looking for the quiz is unavailable at this moment online this man is so pathetic what do you get out of this on Friday I received a letter from a student loan that I paid in full last year they said that I might owe some interest that's a lie they call me to pay the interest and I paid 410.00 dollars with my debit card they told me that if I didn't but I did they even removed that from my credit score student loan from 2010 by law you not even supposed to go back so many years, they were really digging and that was paid in full

Changing the subject this man was also my friend Rosalia this man predator molester I met Rosalia when I was seven so that means you been hunting me down since I was a little girl for no reason at 7 I didn't blame him of anything so he was in that church in school everywhere what is this!I'm terrified of the things that this man is capable to do I forgot to tell you year ago they did me a biopsy is bone narrow they scrap you're a piece of your hip bone and that is so painful you don't take anesthesia there im alive because god is with me they literally had to tight me on the bed and I was screaming years later they wanted to do another one I said no.I'm sharing all of this so you could have a clear understanding of how many things I been through with this psychopath in power how many things they could do to you don't tell me that somebody that loves you is going to do this I can't believe you, love is not about convenience and destruction so let me tell you about my stepfather this man was 12 years younger than my mom they got married after my dad divorce my mom this man since I was a little girl tell lies about me to my mother that I was with some boys went I wasn't he was always following me wherever i was in dr I had boys and girls friend like every other kid because of this man my mom used to beat me I remember one occasion he already in new york, was here so I'm in 125street with some friends it was 3 or 4 girls and he went and told my mom that I was kissing with some girl and that she was in jail

I just met the girl that day my other friend introduce her to me and we was smoking I didn't know that she was in jail it was a lie Im young hanging out when I get home my mom is waiting for me in front of him without even asking me if it was truth she slap me on my face and pulls my hair and hes there watching and laughing she always believe what he said he did that to my other sisters but to me constantly so a man that when I was small did all that and then he got a clone of himself when I was adult to do all of this his also with bye he is a predator that been bothering me and trying to set me up for a lifetime now I understand why he had him as a side

I'm going to add more definitions of what maniac means is an official psychiatric term that meant a patient suffering from mania or maniac disorder involving a euphoric mood and extreme energy someone violent and mentally ill informal a person who behaves in a very wild way no self control whatsoever in other words psychopath is traditionally personality disorder characterized by persistent antisocial behavior,impaired empathy and remorse and egotistical traits a person that been close interaction with a psychopath for a long period of time eventually finds out this person has been using him all along.they are premeditated uncaring everything is a big act he continue because the results that he's getting are not what he wants. Like I said before he calculates every dollar that I make to see how he could continue to rip me off.so let me tell you this whatever I want to do he wants to find someone doing the same thing if I'm writing this book he is with Boca if I want to be astronaut he gets an astronaut this level of hate is insane he doesn't want you to do anything because he doesn't do anything I'm trying to sell my apartment and even the realtor he puts them involve they have to be doing and saying but the purpose is to stop you from your real objective so he wants to get people like thank you a woman that been married to one of my cousins for more then 30 years I don't know that woman and I'm not gay and if I was shes, not my type he gets people like him no job no aspiration, just want to eat drink get high and sleep I don't need that energy next to me I would never consider this person to be in a relationship the first thing you have to do is get your shit together no one is going to take a person clueless without basic stuff get organized stop hating on other people and focus in yourself to better things look at the wrong things you do

I guess I was blind now I see reality and I want to be focus in writing then all this drama and intrigue they love this back and forth and in their game, you never have a choice and is easy to make all this theory to hide the real factor they just waiting for a moment always comparing your situation with other people, and my situation doesn't have to be yours you could be better then me so yours doesn't have to be mine look at a setup at places of employment putting papers from the printer thinking I'm going to take home 2 or 3 pages when I bye the pack of paper in best buy or if I need a little big In the 99cent store they sale a small pack for $1.40 and they also put food and not only regular stuff like the cereal to go little jar lotion that they give for free like if stealing that will solve any problems

I don't have that urge I never been a theft what makes you think I'm going to start now. he wants to say I'm the father of this one the other one what happens when we needed child support money to buy food diapers clothing pay for babysitter pay bills you think I care of someone that totally forgot about us and its nice to come when all the work is done. because you don't like responsibility I'm not playing this mental games especially people in a long term relationship Like I said in my video in my YouTube channel I'm no one's second choice so this man in jersey and all this man here they are in a relationship the clones are single so what you talking about, is pointless now is just a person who clings to another for personal gain especially without giving anything in return, and usually with the implication or effect of exhausting the other resources, parasite, in other words, a person or a thing that takes something from someone or something else and does not do anything to earn it or deserve it, one who habitually takes advantage of the generosity of others without making any useful return.other words that describe simply using the word user! !might be straight forward enough a word which spring to mind for me, due to my locale is a skag also someone who uses another person opportunist freeloader.how do psychopath talk despite their outward arrogance, psychopaths feel inferior to others and know they are stigmatized by their own behavior. Some psychopaths are superficially adapted to their environment and are even popular but they feel they must carefully hide their true nature because it will not be acceptable to others. How you deal with a psychopath try these five strategies keep your emotion in check don't show that you are intimidated don't buy into their story turn the conversation back on them opt for online communication whenever you can don't get confused these people be in good jobs cops surgeons, in media tv etc.1percent of the population,

In Connecticut there is a lot of them out there like this ugly ass nigga that thinks that I'm going to sleep with him ever I don't care who you are to me you could be a millionaire I still don't want you.acting like a bitch the brain of a psychopath is different than other people it has a small prefrontal cortex the part that regulates behavior impulse control and planing in deformed the seat of negative emotions like fear guilt and sadness they are criminals they put a mask of normality that is likable and pleasant they have a history of delinquency no personality ethics they love the chaos they have short term marriage and long terms the difference in the way they think they go further we may get mad and punch somebody their face and that's were it gos, they get mad they want to kill you and they could do it cold with no remorse whatsoever and find a way to cover it.

C

Another type of psychopath Iove narcissist love compliments and lavishly praise anyone who admires or affirms them, the flip side of this coin means that they are extremely sensitive to insults and often respond to criticism with seething rage and retribution they have what psychologist refers to as unstable self-esteem they put themselves in a very high pedestal but it doesn't take much to topple them to the ground what others would perceive as constructive criticism narcissist as a declaration of war.because of their self focused they don't get along with others they have a problem sustaining healthy satisfying relationships so they tend to seek for position of authority where they can work over rather than beside, you colleagues such authority also helps narcissism never blame themselves for their problems is always someone else's fault. He got all this old woman supporting him in all his scams. He fucks old women like my grandmother. That's how old this man is disgusting but I guess he won't have to give anything instead they probably give him. im going through all this that only tells me he's a psychopath using all this old woman for his convenience and they don't see it because they feeling happy somebody is messing them a common trait is parasitic ways they will feed off others people to sustain their lifestyle the more I read about it I get more scared because this guy is literally dangerous this man is bad news.

My god, this is him in all the sense of the word is how you could define a person in articles he wants to monitor people he needs to be monitor on a serious note they capable of anything for their survival sex offenders can look into the victim's face and dominate their will and individually the offenders are not harmed by effective of their behavior because they carried a dark entitlement to rule another person they believe that the victim cannot fight and that you dont know the difference between your person and their needs to dominate you psychopath seek out different type of targets from infants to children to adolescents to adults the predator could be someone who assaults his date his spouse, a young person everyone he has authority over as a priest young pastor teacher or professor the most important thing to sexual predator is to act coercesively and persuasively and out of range of an observer they do this because they are addicted of been predator they can keep victimizing thus they target unsuspecting unexposed people who need them on some manner for grade for coaching or playing time for a potential job or a promotion or for family unity or for financial stability for community acceptances people who pray on others look and act like every one else in fact they often go out of their way to appear trust worthy to gain access to those they seek to victimize.

When a person wants to impose on a person that's wrong I don't want to be under no circumstances why I'm writing this book because I got inspired identifying psychopath I'm also going to translate this books in Spanish I want the Spanish audience to get it too this misery and all the cash that they taken from me and when it comes for them to gives they send petty cash you believe that I don't accept excuses to people that are irresponsible look the people in 181 they have all type of venders they sell from food to earrings hookah sweat beans clothing Etc. and the people that don't have papers they buy a pin and with that, they paid their taxes is initiative of wanting to do something for themselves. screaming so I'm rushing to get him in the building when I came upstairs he only has the undershirt and a green hoodie that he had in the morning no coat, no scarf, no hat a child that is asthmatic and I keep sending him hats they never come back I have to buy several but this when out of hang what my son has to do in who was who as a side look how cold it is thanks god I had an extra coat and hat at the house I told the bus person first I thought it was in the bus but is worse they send him without his stuff on purpose that's some cruel stuff you understand that this person doesn't limit to damage or even to harm a child that been hospitalize lots of times so what is it that your doing this is a kid, this is exactly what im saying this finger don't cares who he hurts this is how you know that they not related to my children why I say that because you wouldn't hurts yours or wont do things to your own Findingo is not related to any of my children that's why he hates them he done shit to everybody that only says he is not the person that had me as a side he contradicts his own self he say one thing and do other that's how I get my answers.this is how you get them he want to hurt me thru anything this child that if i taking a bath in the morning he gets an asthma attack when he feels the cold out side that's why I giving a bath at night so imagine with out his coat and proper gear

What are your intentions.I call the school they apologize but that's not enough what if my son would be hospitalized.you know how I said before everything is connected I found out today that the woman that has an order of protection that made false accusations about me is the bye woman he set this up you understand what's happening here that's the reason his messing her shes a floor behind me you don't have to be rocket scientist trying to figure this out hurt my children my finances everything that involves me so to clear my mind I been working out I start doing a 3 days challenge is going fine so far this was one of my new year resolutions not only to lose some weight is to make it like a routine of life when you get older you need to stay healthy and that's also a stress release with all these problems I need to realize my stress somehow since I am not having sex,so a person that abandons you tells you some many things while you are pregnant you are ugly you're getting so fat I have a new girlfriend I went into a depression after birth coming drunk with lipstick shade in his shirt he told me i hate you me, my child, he even told me that he hopes the city takes him he found my son ugly because he was looking like me we used to fight and he hit me and I hit him too his intentions were to leave like he left me and got more children with another woman I been by myself for seven years all of this is a big setup from the beginning so to be part of figs creepy group your qualifications are you have to be able to mess with her however he thinks that bothers me no at all I want my story to be heard so yesterday a guy from corcoran realty came over to be exact at about 11:00am

He made presentation with his portfolio of different coops and one specific with my address apt number I have to say he gave a good presentation I said I will read it and get back with him but he wants a 6% and to put my apartment at 480,000 with an option of negotiable but his strategy was he sales it fast but Im not looking for a fast sale im looking for a little more my plan is to buy another property so I need a little more and Im not rushing into anything people put you on streets so you could make stupid decisions that you regret later so my decision is no I post a picture of my apartment in facebook page and is listed in Trulia and Zillow im just going to be patient and see what happens Im just putting everything out there like I said everything is connected so to feel a little better i went shopping and got me a couple of shirts and took care of errands i'm trying to live a normal life, if they ask me if is something that you would like to change in my pass I would answer Franklin, Alex,fig, Charlie to be honest everyone this guys really mess up my life a whole bunch of ghost and I want to repair all the damage they made I want to be a new grace I think I still have a chance I look young and I like to work and now that my girls are big we really could do this together if they want but my main focus is helping myself and others to identify the psychopaths so I been researching and studies indicates that in Connecticut is that number one state that have more psychopath but New York is number four state,they are in the political environment

They have lives, family jobs and business,leaderships positions their Christmas builds professional network there are very convincing people to invest or believe in their product how they gain control manipulating emotions they use intimidation tell sob stories they view their lover as a tool possession or someone who validates their personality because they share similar view their relationship turn toxic fear abandonment and the inability to bond trails insensitivity negative emotions behaviors until the relationship is destroy I'm going to continue with more,do psychopath know what they doing? Yes, they do at the start of the relationship they are known for presenting themselves as the ideal partner so the victim fall in love with them very quickly this involves behaving a certain way for weeks or months including complements doing nice things spending lots of time with the victim also making a good impression on a family and friends they present themselves as happy carefree friendly helpful and later on after some level of commitment

Their behavior changes they are always right don't accept responsibility for their mistakes they will blame others quickly for any bad happening how long does recover from a psychopath takes? Some time and a therapist. Yes, I'm going to seek one as soon as possible don't think it is your fault you're set to lose in this type of relationship. Let me tell you how the creep squad works if they have a fat woman they start doing all type of witchcraft so you could gain weight instead of putting their woman in a diet they want to deform you if they don't work they want to get you fired if some of them are on drugs they want to make you a junky or theft from doing witchcraft so your hair doesn't grow or fall off do you understand instead of them changing for the good they want to convert you in a bum or bad news for society so you could be in their level and misery even doing witchcraft so you lose your mind no one that wants to make me worse have me as a side I want people that are a blessing. in my life that I feel better as a person and no is not sexually not worse like this guy that I talk at work and so many people the guess I enjoy talking to all of them.

Changing the subject the good thing about myself I'm self discipline if I have to stay without eating just to get back to my weight I will do it I don't need to become another person for anybody if you are retarded without employment in the streets, no I'm not that i been stable, im my own person I make my own decision and I definitely hate the rushing see what I mean the one that all he did is use me and send a clone to me I used to wonder why he doesn't reason his not real all this was a conspiracy and you know what's crazy that they all hate me I couldn't do harm to all these people at the same time something is wrong here I came to the conclusion it could be my step-dad a man that did all type of harm to me and my sisters always getting us in problems is one more thing one time I was living in 125stmorning side and is like midnight as I go up the stairs I hear screaming a woman voice but is downstairs in the basement i look at the window is open and I look down I see this woman bend over and hes doggie style position it was dark put I still recognize him so I go one more floor down and he is messing that woman in her ass I go get my mom because one she was a crack-head

I said to my self this dirty man could get my mother sick she went down stairs and caught them she chaise the woman and she throw him out of the house look at that he was always chasing people and when he got discover hes mad I told my mom because he was messing in the same building with a crack head im thinking for my moms safety not because he was messing really i didnt care but at the same time he dont have respect.moving forward January 21, so today I decided to go to the gym and after the gym, I went to several stores to buy and pay some bills first I went PC to get josh a tablet and I got me shredder then I went to jimmy jazz got me my uggs that I needed and stop at spectrum and pay my cable bill my makeup finish so I stop at mac store to get my foundation powder and my sin lipstick that I like buy my cosmetics there so basically I know the prices I noticed my bill was kind of high for three things I paid but I said to my self when I get home I'm going to take a look at this carefully and that's what I did

I see 3times they put 31 dollars I only bought 2things for 31 one dollars I'm writing this just to give you an example of what I'm saying they always trying to find a way to screw me over like lately I been throwing out the receipt they thought I wasn't going to look and throw it out and is the same with my rent because he is trying to find a way of how he could take advantage a total psychopath mentality so I went back the next day to mac and show the woman that took care of me she said she didnt notice she was nervous I said miss is ok it could happen

Listen I know that is the finger I dont blame no one they have do what he says is not only there is every where if I go to the supermarket i need to put attention so they dont ring twice or more just for I could pay more money any place restaurants movie theater even bills is so messed up his intentions are totally evil for instances I never been with Cesar or the eye this man make up this prophecy and add this person and they hunt you down for no reason they really want you to believe there bullshit theory I found a paper that he had and he was explaining in details that they were going to start every thing in January of the new year

The people they needed to participate they really time me it been 9 long years of a constant harassment I was 34 years old when this start every where I go everything was set up.so you understand he had to do what he was told or plan to change the topic I recently change the locks but they got the new key, they steal from little things in my house Joshua shoes I'm telling you these people do too much from invading my privacy touching my belonging when I'm not home I don't understand what is the issue

He really thinks which I'm sure he had him as a side if he pregnant me I have to pay him isn't the opposite man pay child support when they pregnant a woman I'm lost here because this man thinks he needs to be rewarded like you need to pay for not being an in responsible person or this $360.a month that you recently started giving this think this is cash to support a child. look how they build their fortune they freeload eat for free at their different mate get freebies from people old lady sleep in the different house so if something goes wrong they have another victim if you are an old lady they eating their food stamps or Section 8 program, or housing if you a taxpayer they saving their money in the bank living out of you no responsibility whatsoever so off course they could get rich like that

C

Let me ask you a question If you dating a handicapped person and more respect for them is alright but I don't have to become handicapped is not my condition no I'm my own person and I have my own issues and when I'm saying this I'm just paraphrasing and they could be overweight or other conditions this is an example is not that anyone is handicapped but look at the mentality the woman that is wide open instead of looking for a doctor to close her they get a guy clone with a big penis why you think is the purpose here? to destroy other woman's pussy because hers is already destroyed evil and creepy.

The women are men and the man are a women is all a scam that's their purpose he really wants to marry all his clones, fig is a big enemy to fight, to be honest, is difficult to win this person they only want to make and don't let others cash because that's a form of controlling and manipulation also so they could call you a bump you are worse than me except very miserable and egotistical all they send me was their clone so he's mad because I cheated on his clone that's not a person when you live a life thinking you going to be young forever one day you wake up to reality living like there is no tomorrow with your children and with everyone around.

You going to be a very lonely old man or woman never thinking for others or helping just being reckless and in the milestone stages for life, reality is going to hit you when are you going to realize? don't blame others for your mistakes fixed them. I'm working on mine and trying to be a better human been how can everything I do affects you how can that be, your theory is lame I'm working in the thing I want in my life I have to admit that in all this process may me realize that I don't need anyone to make me happy.

I'm working in the inner self things that were damage inside and I didn't any about, for example, my problem trusting people and the way I feel about a man if you have me as aside what you want me to do? Trying to set me up and putting me in jail is your way of saying you had me as a side. Your purpose is very obvious and even my children are suffering. All you do is always looking for an advantage and you really think you could get away with it. That's how they get peoples funds putting you in jail freezing your account using power look what they doing to Noemi making her pay out of pocket for classes first they made her paid $2000 and now because she doesn't have health insurance what health insurance has to do with getting a student loan she has to pay more money by semester and he's telling me his the father that's a lie is that he knows that she had $5,000dollars

So he wants to take it making her pay a lot more of what she has to pay. They don't want to give her financial aid. I'm telling you everything is to take from us everywhere they can. I'm not rich. Why don't you go to the rich person or somebody else because he's not giving anything so instead of blaming us we are an easy target for you that's so fucked up. Listen to this if you are married all your clones are still you so they not single they're yourself so get your facts together these people are more hungry then you to take your money or the minimum so when you encounter one of this psychopath they examine you don't think because they have money they ready to share and live a good life remember pretending is their strategy for getting victims.

Every day he shows his real motor his intentions especially trying to stop others from growing you want to know a real sign they want to get you in a situation so you could get fired some of them hate employment he hits the trump so he wants to see what he could get away what getting my refund have to do with who you dating changing the subject is people that think that they are the only ones entitled of getting things and making good choices in life that's so wrong I believe that the sun comes out for everyone.you have to understand this is a sign of controlling that's the reason they have all this commotion and the main purpose is cover. pay me back everything that you stole from me and that's how I know that was you.

There are people in this world that knowing them is a blessing and their others diabolically and they persecute you forever very creepy so this man in power set this up and he sends all these creepy people after me I haven't slept with any of them look at this, man they are in their house with their wife and kids and send a clone to me because his intentions were to rob me to see how he could get some money that's all it was, however you want to put it, loving this man has cost me a lot of things is incredible but I'm not filling my heart with resentment and anger and hate for no one, I love everybody and I learn to accept people the way they are if a millionaire has me as a side and is no difference in my life why I want to be with them is nothing good happening instead they want me to be in misery that's why I preferred to be by myself and do my own thing.

Some of this millionaire only think about themselves and if you think you getting something you are wrong they more hungry then you to take what is yours instead of helping you look in this problem this man sending a few dollars of child support but has spent more in this set up hunting me persecuting me an drama.my message to everyone is sometimes you could get better results with regular people that work hard and want to accomplish things with you than with this millionaire they want everything for themselves.some people get with you for the wrong reason so let me tell you something that happened recently I when to remove the IUD they send me to do sonogram 96 street they send them the sonogram results they still couldn't take it out the IUD what the other place did was they cut the strings so I have to go into surgery

But to remove this, was a very simple procedure I had this before not the marina but the metal one the 10 years I went on my period it took about five minutes the doctor remove it with no pain this is some criminal shit, why I'm saying criminal because he's sending people from doctors to cut my strings so I could go under anesthesia the intentions were evil in all the senses of the word, why they have to do all of this fig is capable of killing and then say it was an accident look how deep they go into shit this man was opening me with all does utensils to open my pussy that was the purpose I been solvent for almost two years and now this procedure I was bleeding so much this man wants my things public capable of hurting anyone kids adults anyone that he feels is obstacle that interferes with his purpose as soon as I come out of my house he starts a hunting process so everyone has their life with their family and kids but they continue to mess with me why is that? They have some nerves and want to put people under stress for anything I don't have to be with no one my intentions are to work in making my money like getting the new job and continue writing my life stories they so focus on me and im not into them so instead of their woman look for a solution of closing her pussy they got man clones to open woman's pussy because their wide open evil people he thinks im falling for his game he has all this mental games they not working, I read a letter that this guy had here he was saying that in January of the new year they was going to start how many people he needed for this plan he was detailing everything that's why he left.

it was meant to be like that's the way they build their fortune is living of peoples at different mates so he could be out of responsibility if you want to know where Im at writing this im hyatt centric I came at 3:44pm i was trying to buy a coffee in Starbucks and my account was frozen I wasnt able to do so im working with kerling another guard that works for mg shes at the elevator entrance and im at bar/restaurant entrance is Friday evening slow traffic of people in the lobby the guess go to the restaurant for two reasons one to eat and drink and two to get an access card to go to lounge at the 54 floor im writing this just to let you know that inspiration comes from everywhere you are at

Changing the topic this man watch a lot soap operas he really things that man is going to go with me and run away omg hes doing what he likes nobody wants him look at this I made a transfer of $80 and the bank only gave me $65.00 im missing $15.00 they dont have an explanation they need to put my money back I have to said they return it in my account petty stuff like this that im talking about fig that's why he hates me so much and is funny but im really praying that his man messes up with another woman to see what they going to say now it wasn't me how many things this man can get away with.why you want to involve me with people that are not doing anything for themselves this is like a terror movie this person is so evil they live worse then a very poor person they chain inside all your demons are flowing all over him why he got all these people after me because the scam that he wanted to do got interrupted his admitting in public he stole my cash they love to screw peoples lives because theirs is not going anywhere this set up took him years and dedication I give him that he decided to destroy my life people are taking this as a joke but he hates me so much that he wants me dead when you come with a check of damages and prejudices then I will listen to you mean while no they want to get their way or else and they still have the nerve to say they had me as a side,when you see people criticizing so much they trying to hide themselves so is better to expose you them to fix my act so you know whats, I have been on my feet the whole night in the job

So this man starts messing with you like you don't have nothing to do like your feet don't hurt I had to take a cab at 79street to come home the other day because of his nonsense changing the subject I been in a challenge of losing weight I weigh myself im 188 ponds my goal is 155 like I said in my YouTube video I just want to lose 5ponds every month Im not rushing is until July so I have enough time why?I'm doing it like this so the weight could stay off and I do this like a life routine I'm missing a few more for this month 2 ponds for this month so today I'm taking laxatives to go to the bathroom that really helps so your stomach get in the habit of shrinking little by little this is one of the little things that I do to keep me distracted and not think so much about this stuff that's happening his intentions where to get me deported messed up my kids life me in the streets something very tragic one of the things that the spit told me was he builds from here and there his money he was trying to say they take from the taxes payers and robbing peoples, so everyone is against me why you want to hate in a woman that is trying everyday you already made your money let others get theirs or at least trying to, I choose to forgive why is not about the person is about me I free my soul and all the bitterness disappears I don't want to carry resentment and baggage of all the bad things that happened to me when I was a kid till now.

You start seeing the world with another perspective I have ton of people that I would hate but I chose not to I forget and forgive so god could forgive me of all my sins help me move forward in life believe me I have so much inside that with this problem everything came out of me things I didn't event know it was there hurting me inside now I understand why I had trust issues and so much pain inside when Im mad I say things I don't mean I could even insult people but as soon as that gos away im normal and I could even talk to that person and I don't wish them bad god knows in other words I don't hold grudges so look at this I watch movies now they doing movies according to their advantage like nothing about paying all the cash that they stole instead they going with all bullshit theory that don't make no sense because I was the pregnant one that went to nine months of pregnancy went into labor and i know who I slept with off course you want to look for woman or people in rooms like the napkin a homeless don't know where she's going in life and don't have no money she is looking for any circumstances to take advantages that's all she knows how to survive

she is clueless, the crazy part is that she thinks nothing is wrong so when you find people like that what can you think about them shes a psychopath so of course every time you hungry and don't have no money shes going to hate me I don't know this people is not only her is a lot of people with that mentality instead of doing things for themselves they are waiting for or a movie that mentions them so they act is all and act opportunity but god watching you then you want to blame the world for what's happening in your life you bring this karma to your life so please be aware of your surroundings is people ready to infiltrate in your circle of friends and people that you love or they part of it be wise and observe the only thing that the sniffer wants is to destroy my family he hates me so much that is he is fig he wakes up every day with new plans how to destroy my life the world knows he don't sleep he's is constantly watching me is something unbelievable I should be hating you and i'm not I don't want to waste time on that i'm a free spirit. changing the topic I was talking to my tax guy Efrain I know him for a few years now so he wants to move to Spain and he been there several times his son went to school in Barcelona and everything he loves it there he's planning to retired life there I told him that I want to visit the place this new year I might consider that too he said in dr you can't leave is too much delinquency going on, to be honest, I love dr but I won't move there one because I leave here my whole life I told him that i'm half from Spain from my dad side, so he was giving me an, advised that I could apply for residency in Spain and they will give it to me

Because i'm a Spaniard descendant lets see what happened this man hates the fact that I get any cash I see his game when you stopping me I don't know Cesar was a guard that works at Citi I don't know anything else about him like the other guard Almonte, Ramsea,Tiggs, Cristina, so many people I work with that doesn't mean anything we didn't do anything some of them we hang out on happy hours after work and that's it like people at this job we were co- worker that's all.

look at the end of the day what should matter to you is to pay me back no one what so ever is going to enter into no agreement when they owe her money the first step to take is pay me everything that you stole from me that's the first step anyone will take I'm not stupid until I see at least a part of my finance that you stole nothing that you saying or doing has no meaning to me useless you know how hard it is for me to put my cash together so you could feel untitled of stealing my stuff is not right so I'm focusing my energy in things that make sense to me you guys not making no sense.

Set this job to one of my co-workers I'm focused at the place I write but when the lobby is empty or when I talk to one guess and they talk to me about something reminded me of things that I did or one of my experiences, that's how I get a little inspiration here and there if you look at my scrapbook is a lot of scrabbles but from that, I take the important things is like hints of stuff that goes to your brain then I write it in my computer I'm giving you inside hints how you write a book I believe that if I could do it everybody could do it too I'm fighting this once and for all nobody is worth going thru all the things I been throw how people that you don't know is going to revenge you for what? Is it a little odd I guess I was blind to think that we were going to end up together and be a happy ending a rock n roll fan and I was r&b hip-hop a little bit of everything but open-minded about other music I start liking rock and even dancing merengue old songs when I met them his part of my memory is a sad ending but fig is not letting that happen is ok because I'm ready to go and start my new life in a new place anywhere from Spain to any place in the world and his, not part of it these people watch a lot of soap operas he thinks one day we going to run away like in the novels

Now he's doing what he likes and I'm doing what I like working in his Tobacco lounge and I'm happily writing my story. People get carried away with things that are not real you know what I was going to delete my social media again but then I said to my self no im not letting no one dictate in my life and I want people to know me so why should I have to do this to please others no,Im pleasing my self and while im analyzing my life at this age I'm still struggling from the bad that want to stop me from growing as a human been and doing positive things in my life for no reason im really tired of this bullshit you know they are digging into my life looking for anything everyday im in a battle with strangers because fig wants to mess with me they all his lovers this man puts my own mother against me.

I have to say many things have happened in my life in this 43 years like it wasn't enough the shit that I been throw.let me change the topic for a little, I recommend you to match your 401k that important,to think about the future don't live today only don't spend more of what you make save some money for retirement even in credit cards don't pay the minimum don't be afraid of the unknown perhaps you should plan your future get your priorities straight work hard get people with your same ideas goals you could build a good future for your self like that be honest dont pretend something that your not if is possible say less then what you are is better to surprise people then bragging.

Good morning today, it's Sunday morning i'm on hyatt centric is 7:40am in the morning got here early they have another event the marathon was yesterday we have the Irish parade the street are crowded of people and cops im at my post the lobby looking outside we have a slow traffic of guess coming in I thing some of the guess from here are going to the parade, I'm just giving you my daily routine at the job im all my thoughts today i'm going to give you a little more details of what i'm doing while im writing this book is February,03,20 my son Josh having surgery we got there about 8:50 am they register him everything when well the only problem was that at 6:00am I told the nurse he ask me for milk and since is a routine I give him milk like before school every morning

I totally forgot that they told me no food before midnight so we had to wait until 2:30pm to go into surgery the surgery lasted 49minutes it went well the baby was in recovery they gave him pain medicine we got out of the hospital stop to get Motrin and triple antibiotic ointment pain relief for josh I got him soup and milk juice and some pampers for his surgery now we in the recovery mode at least he's not in pain his playing and watching videos i'm exhausted here im going to bed early I spoke to a lady that told me about a variety of services to help josh with his slide autism and i'm going to read the paper work and may be request some of the services for him let's see what happens next for today i'm going to bed I feel like it was me in that surgery room my body is beet till the next time.

Now that I'm going back thinking of things in my past and when people used to ask me Grace why the guys you date die you kill them? I said no and smile but it hurt so much inside Michelle's dad, when I was seventeen , Noemi's dad, Michael, an ex boyfriend; Patricia's dad didn't die but he went away to Europe and never help me or her till this date i send her to Europe one time she only lasted a month and half she wanted to come back right away. At the end of the day im under the impression this person wants to get rewarded for supposing pregnant me and not pay child support with none of this kids look at Noemi he knows she's upstate in school and she needs cash to eat for her personal stuff because she's studying why if he saying his the father why he cant send her something no instead he is bothering me constantly don't even care about my child well being Joshua in surgery and they sending people to the hospital for their plan I don't understand. Josh had circumcision surgery it was to take a little bit of skin this people peal his little penis that's so swollen that im scared of any infection last night i couldn't sleep just making sure he's fine changing his diaper putting the antibiotic on the diaper also giving him Tylenol every 3an half hours and Motrin I switch it up today I got him pull ups overnight they are stronger absorb the urine i got him large size so the area have space in between he's feeling much better. They want to say it's this one the other one no one is helping me or giving me back the money that they stole from me that's the reason I don't put no mind of what they saying the first step that any person take is helping should be is giving back what they stole from me.

Now going back to the topic so what is that you want to prove everybody noticing that you are a jealous evil man that don't know what to do and they all in a relationship but want to stop me from doing my life how can that be base your theory in other people's stuff never on yours always basing on another person life event is very scary the fact that this person doesn't care and do things publicly and I guess his in power so he's allowed of doing all type of things he's not supposed to, always threatening people with everything and anything, psychopath are always planning their next plan of setups

These people are criminal minds always trying to make you say things you don't mean or do implicate you in their game I'm going to give you more examples from people holding grudges since teenager or less than that, gather all of them together I never seen that in my whole life they mention names and place of things that I don't even remember them

How can they be trying to stop every movement that you want to do and all his theory is that his with someone that is irrelevant to me is none of my business who you with or what you do especially is not willing to help me restore my cash my business is to help my kids the one that need me more and get my life organized I feel that I wasted too much time in things that at the end wasn't worth It didn't get nothing good you don't have anything have dignity and shame that's what I have nobody that is in a relationship is talking shit to me they making up a situation and a conflict no foundation that's why they needed so many people to make this scam he made me believe im in a relationship and that i was his wife and marry me was made up name and date of birth of another person that's why he don't have emotions for my kid they really thought they was going to get away with that he didn't want to put his last name to the child that wasn't the plan.

Its true that you can't change the past but the future yes, I could be with other people and do my thing you blame me for falling in love with a man when i'm a little girl, now I understand that this been my biggest error if I only knew then what i know now, it would be different thing fig is the one that hates me. when you understand the process of differencing people then you would know the difference every person is unique in his own way so fig do this sleep with this people and convert them in my enemy without me knowing everyone shares the same feelings hate, back a guy that I saw out there in the street on this block and just had a few short conversations one of them was that I was looking for a person to rent my place and I ask him if he knew somebody that I could rent the place conversations as a neighbor so now he was with fig also he has his wife and kids that I have seen him with them for a long time seems he been in this block so you understand the maniac that I'm dealing with from getting people fake identifications different date of birth two names convince this just to scam a person this is like police work is too many details

People from jail this man is sick you did it when I was 23when I already had 3 years with a life insurance policy you wanted to get my life insurance I had 3 years with it and now when I was 33 years old my house and my life insurance and my cash, this guy the other day said he has life insurance and your excuse is because of him i wasn't even thinking about him both of the time you made me believe i got married I was trying to do my life so you understand their level of hate. I understood that man move on a long time ago I haven't seen him or heard from him I ask for him but that was that, for years i let that go i'm not a maniac. that been your excuse to rip me off

You saw potential in me and you been doing this for a long time that's why the guys that have fake identification and fake date of birth so when everything gets done it be no trace martin had a different name this also is not a coincidence this man saw that i was 19 but always thinking about my future and he decided that was going to rob my things creating all of this people and this scenarios to scam me a single woman trying, that was raising three little girls by myself with no help of a father but in your demented mind you saw an opportunity of advantage and you know what made me think about a life insurance as such a young age because the father of my children keep dying and they stayed with anything no social security benefit anything just me busting my ass so I said to my self I want to get something that if something happens to me they at least have something from me they count on because is no father or family in the father side Of course I was all they have I wanted us to have things I still do to this day that's the reason I get up every day and Im writing this book I want to be an inspiration of not giving up and trying everyday of making a difference in my life and if i could in others too.

So a man that never help me with the children ever not even instead he wants to stop me from getting a good job any thing that is about progress he don't care I know for a fact that he making all this they want to make me believe people i never slept with has me as a side that's why they made this lie this man to make me believe something, you understand how evil this people could be and I guess is not enough they had destroy my life for 33 years that's a life time of lies and set up what I done to you so bad that you feel that you need to continue messing my life up for no reason why so evil? Look even if that only god know I just need them to let me do what I got to do with my life so you think by saying this that i'm going to stop writing that only is going to make me write more so people could understand how evil this person could be and how they could set you up so.

According to him i'm not entitle of to get money i'm in entitled to buy a house to write this book to better myself this man evil and have so much envy that he thinks he puts envy in me seen my kids doing better that's what I always wanted but in your mind you are crazy all of them Michelle Patricia Noemi josh I want them to get good jobs that's the purpose of studying and I'm writing and studying for my insurance test.

You not making me feel no kind of way that's how you feel towards me. I know that God has things for me so I don't envy no one my blessing are coming I believe that off course you want to bring the worse type of people so you could feel important person, in other world, using them for his purpose that's the way they feel good about himself that's is disgusting a nasty cheap and this other person always looking for chaos things that im not worry about that is happening is like hell you don't know whats hitting you this are psycho and they base their lives in lies is the bye he is a freeloader always looking for advantages

Changing the topic today Feb 07, my daughter Noemi came from school on the bus for the weekend to see josh she came upstairs play a little with josh and when she came back downstairs I gave her some cash she said she was hungry im happy shes here so she could help with josh tomorrow morning when I go to work been here for 5 days straight and on Tuesday he has a doctors appointment i'm thinking of sending him on Wednesday after the doctor gives the ok he does feel better it still a little swollen but is better then before the first day was after the surgery i was scared and worried the good thing is that he pee normally and he eating normally but he still have a discomfort he walks funny and with pull ups he's afraid of touching it is normal even though I put the medicine in the diaper,

C

Getting back to topic this individuals are so weird that they don't know what to do im here writing and thinking and they acting like his coming on his motorcycle and taking me with him or something this people are so weird I want to ask them? what I'm doing that you guys acting like this is tons of cars outside every day and people on the street walking and doing all type of signals I made a shirt saying that I dont care who you have as side and im making more shirts according to the to problem I think they like this gets me agitated and to be honest when my nerves are hype I talk to myself they doing all this witchcraft to me that fucks your nervous up but is normal is like a little thinking out-loud you know when you are crazy when you answer your self Im not there I want the world to know how this people do they done this before to other people. I learn to ignored it now doesn't bother me no more

I know the plan also they do all they prophecy with my things they had everything well plan this is like a terror movie the more you find out the more you get scared I admit for people that can understand me they probably think I'm a little crazy but in a good sense they have crazy stupid im crazy smart and I'm not afraid of the unknown instead I want to know what's happening I consider my self a little curious I think that you have to be a little, I'm a true believer in been myself not pretend something that I'm not, this man is so fake he act like he don't care about your life but behind your back his doing all type of things to stop you from obtaining employment a house whatever you want to do he wants to be the only one accomplishing things and the others mess up that's so wrong provoking incidents to get you arrested so you get a record and your life be all screw up his excuse was that I gave him the letter when I was thirteen

I could only change my future not my past im going to continue with my life but I needed to tell my story since thirteen to now it been 33 years of set ups however want to put it out there so what are we discussing here I don't want to be with no one but for a long time this people been messing my future up and they even send people saying to me thank you for helping me like is a joke that they stole my money and you acting like a maniac because I wasn't even thinking like that for him.

You act like his the only man in this world. Psycho! He thought that by me finding out they together I was going to commit suicide or something when the bible says *maldito el hombre que confia en otro hombre* curse be a man that believe in another man word I don't even want him but I need to say my story is part of my life and he wants to make me believe something that I know for a fact he's acting like is nobody else in this world fig his desperate this man been trying to mess my life up till this day because this people are capable to do to a 13 year old girl I needed to find out I feel I deserve that closure in my life with this situation and all the evil things they did to me

Who plan this? Like I said before you can change the past the only thing you could change is the future does are call experiences specially for someone conveniences just because they wasn't part of it and i'm going out of the topic because I just need to express my feelings if I was with a man that left me for another woman he wasn't meant to be that's the way I see things and god has better things for my life. I guess everyone has a price to pay and some are going to be tempted. What's your price to sell out the prophet of God? Its funny but when this process started I said those words and people were getting jobs trips and so many things just for recording me at the train wherever I went.

I have to say I survive because I put my trust in god moving forward in this time and age. I preferred to do whatever it makes me happy going to a nice restaurant or the movie theaters going to a play shopping hanging out with my daughters not been around people that take out the worst of me I'm not doing that to myself I don't need anyone that doesn't contribute. It's funny how sometimes we ask for time when we want to be with other people or the relationship is broken when you don't want to continue but don't have the Guts to say it is better to say time to explore with the next person and if it doesn't work out you could always come back or if you realize it was an illusion

I have another question why he is so important that everyone has him as a side? Something to think about and another thing who's proud of somebody cheating on them so he put it on music videos in movies something is wrong here. Is a lot of men out here that are single so when I want to get back in a relationship is not a problem I consider myself fun to be with, personality wise interesting.

Nice personality fun to talk to never had a problem when it comes to man and want to better my self a little cute sexy I'm sorry but I have a lot of good qualities I hope that you don't find me arrogant I dont have to be with people that I don't want to be going to the topic you know why they mad because I scape from them I don't need to be with anyone that I don't like or make me feel uncomfortable

I been working on my thing here at home and at the job let me tell you something you know what happens to people with masters, doctorates degrees, etc they don't believe in God and always looking for logical explanation, mother nature making theory etc but God is about the impossible when men say they cant that's when God starts technical beat the wise is biblical God was going to embarrass the wise with normal technical people

All they need is a prophet of God and his anointing and people to believe is hard to accept the truth I believe in a god that makes impossible to be possible happen and when I say that I mean it in my illness everything that involves my life the kids life this is not a man is Jesus Christ and the holly ghost like the bad is out there also the good I preferred god in my life is people with witchcraft that want to stop you from been you is that they hate god in you they want to take him out of you is something that is unbelievable and this book is not about religion

At the same time I want people to understand God is real bring him in your life make him part of you he could inspired you for things that you want to do, they are people so greedy that they become another person to get your things is the bye a woman/ man that been marry to my cousin for more then 30 plus years recently they just got a divorce so you became a guy to mess me over not for her husband Juan that we never had an incident I never said or did anything so she is real criminal

l want to start with people never had a problem with your husband but for him and to try to steal my stuff the more the truth comes out the more I be horrified but for some people that never been part of your love is convenient to act or try to ignore whatever is not convenient because they wasn't part of your past that never happen that's how they act like your situations your kids your live don't exist because they wasn't part of it and the people with clones they are part of you but is not you is like having a kid he's like you but they are another person

I want to enjoy my experience my life and my things I want my kids to enjoy too but im still young and strong I never understood of people trying to live throw other people another thing when you are worried about a person getting five thousand ten thousand dollars you envy that anybody that works could save that amount and more so you have less then that's? why you envy anything people get instead of making your own I guess you don't have the source.or you preferred not too, of things that I accomplish working what is it that when it comes to me is a problem these people are very unhappy with themselves

On valentine day, I made myself happy just going in a restaurant and wearing something new I learn to make myself happy don't need no one to make me feel anything you know that these people are so evil that just because I want to lose weight that bothers them in what that affects you or if I say I like someone if you are jealous of me for your man and I like another person I think you should be happy at least you don't have me as competition so your stuff is pure evil now that I'm writing and finding out the truth about everything I don't know if you understand I need closure with him to it was a lot of people involved to hurt me and got me in a situation who idea was it? You got to understand I want to know why they all hate me so much that letter made him millions thats the answer instead you should be happy that god inspired me for him.

Changing the topic so far I had lost 11pounds in two months so the challenge is working I'm happy about that I still have a lot more 20 more to go the three days working out and reducing the portions of food it works with plastic wrapping another method that I use is writing what I eat for breakfast lunch and dinner in between eating an apple grapefruit, and strawberries, tangerines watermelon,banana,that help reduce anxiety you could have that instead of sweets so you could have a count and you count paragraph8calories I'm sharing my life in this book so you could understand that I'm a normal woman that this group of people wanted to damage for the purpose of obtaining my belongings the sniffer is the medium the blujo he doesn't have anything to do with me that's why he hates on normal things he living a limited life on a checks this man is sick he doesn't know what to do to leave me alone

When I'm not home they sending people here to steal my personal belonging shirts shoes and more they really think because I have a lot of stuff I'm not going to notice what's missing this man is so demented I had guess in the hotel that im working telling me that the sniffer the elevator come upstairs that he wants people to believe hes me some stranger that leaves in a room he wants to leave in my house and he be here touching my things he is insane I don't care who had him as a side they need to leave me out of that I don't know this man and he was doing or still sleeping with all this old woman including my mother so she could help him obtaining his goal the more I find out things the more I be thinking how this crooks chase you down to see how they could get and use any excuse you was dealing with my boyfriend they are theft that's what they do like Cesar the sniffer why this man don't leave me alone I don't have nothing to do with this man they send people here to tell me Cesar the trump I don't care because I wasn't with him they creating this scenario you understand why they needed me to be crazy

Because if my mind is mess up I wouldn't know what was true or lie they was thinking im going to mess this woman's life to obtain her things everybody knows what you are doing he needs to stop this man wants to compare me with the worse I guess that's how he feels good about himself people without employment and not trying to get one I don't even waste my time with people like he always comparing me with this people don't have anything to do with me or what I want to do with my life I been thinking of going to new jersey for a long time about fifteen years now to be honest I didn't know he was out there but even where I want to go is a problem Im free I could make my decisions what they want is to keep messing with me in everything that im doing this man hates me and wants to destroy me he is looking for any excuse to destroy us. He is a delinquent with money and all his done is destroy peoples lives

This man needs to be stop his tactic is to put intrigue and gossip she said this about you so you got to do? something about it that's the mentality I don't know no man in a room the guys that I been they had there apartment so stop bringing all this maniacs that I don't know who they are this man till this day I don't understand why he hates me so much we had sex one two times the same day that was the only time and after he left I had to throw away the bed it was infested with bed bugs it was tons and tons of them so sleeping with him something that I don't do in my house with this guy in my bed cost me $3500 dollars I had to get rid of it do you think I want to be with some one like that he has to be dealing with woman all screw up no one has to decided for me

I choose who I want to be with is not what is convenient to another person because they are homeless or don't want to get a jobs or what ever the reason no,I don't want him anymore but I want to find another person that have the qualities that im looking for in a man all the problem i got into just for loving him he could be my kids father it doesn't matter anymore I feel I have a chance to find some one who loves me and respect me he could stay together with fig they could even move together is alright I realize I need to leave him in my past, like everybody else

This has been horrible; this jealous man that doesn't leave me alone thinking I want to be with his man I was blind or I just didn't know you can't blame me of something that I'm not aware of that you had him as a side a shameless man fig hates me is not right to use that excuse to mess up my personal stuff doesn't have anything to do with whatever I want to do everybody is noticing your plan is always to take something even people in the streets they like this guy hates you they come to my home when I'm at work they don't have any type of respect even dough, I have a camera the camera records when I'm home not the opposite way.

Sometimes I notice is pre-recorded how is that I don't have an explanation the man in power he wants to make-believe his waiting for me to mess I been my myself seven years now so of what you blaming me now? no boyfriend nothing and he probably messing every day this man think I'm going waist my little bit of youth that I still have after someone is not worried about me if he was he would help me by now no I'm not stupid I know the trump has him as a side and he's always going to choose the trump

He' fig was the one that' use to punch me jealous of this man why you think his with bucca they had a normal life and the clone was bolo how he was five kids with bucca I was a job for him is insane they have their normal life and wanted to destroy mine. he makes his own conclusion and I wasn't even thinking about what you making stuff in your mind sometimes I say a guy is cute I do it on purpose because they need to leave me out of that I have suffered a lot only God is my witness he wants to destroy me for no reason.

I'm not competing for my priority I want to be with someone that doesn't know anybody from my past because I'm not doing that.you was right I needed to erase all my memories now I'm going to do so, this man put the whole family Matos against me but it's ok I apologies to them in my first book, you know why he did that because he knew I care about this person this man destroy every person I ever care about old or young was all this necessary not in my belief I don't have one friend left. they have a drama outside it doesn't matter to me what is reality what I'm writing here

Look at this, I don't have to be with him but I don't need to with people that I don't like and that guy don't have a day off every day with that brown uniform or he won't have any clothing always with that uniform and looking all sweaty the only building he goes into the projects to take packages I think he makes that up he doesn't even work in no ups he wants to give that impression at all hour he is eating in a restaurant with the same uniform at three in the morning the same something is wrong with him jealous sending people after me and doing All types of things like today I'm going up the stairs after the gym one of the daughters of the woman that I had the incident she's coming down and looks at me and shows me her phone I hit the trump who cares but all he wants is to confront me with them the same family.

Where he came from don't ask me he hits the trump that's what he said and has him as a side I have seen him here in the block a few times and in one of the days in my aunt's house he told me one day all of you guys have alot of coops I look at him like is non of your business he wants my house because my ex had him as a side what that has to do with my life I think sometimes it has to be the sniffer or somebody else fig that sends these guys, to me his the trump a whole bunch of strangers I'm their target is something unbelievable I don't bother this man I can't understand why you have to do all this to me is not what's convenient to you Cesar never had sexual relations with Grace.

I had an emergency surgery that doesn't mean I been with him they love to make the prophecy of my things they should be in jail that's why I don't copy anyone because I would know the errors, I want to know what I'm doing wrong or right so I could fix it when you busy doing what others do you cant see your mistakes how can you learn from them? Something to think about so lately I been telling guys and woman I think you are pretty or handsome in my understanding I don't see anything wrong with that if you are you ugly I call it how it is that doesn't mean? that I'm going to sleep with you or I want everything that I see I don't want to go to bed with I'm not a freak is very simple you are not the person that I thought you were.

Leave me alone let me move on with my life and I'm saying this to him to everyone the was somebody else I want to live just having fun and being myself with my good thing working to fix my bad thing but always keeping my essence who I'm and what I want to be and you saying want to be? you too old for wanting to be but I feel that if you have strength and determination with hard work is no age limit of what you want in life just focus and do it I want to buy a house I want to go to Europe I want to continue writing my books I have the next titles line up I also want to see if I could go to college so you understand nobody is waiting for me I think I could do this for self-accomplishments

I want to get the insurance job look at so many things that I want to buy an annuity for my future so I don't outlive my assets. you see the sky is your limit buy other things property if I could help people in need with the profit from my book sales go on trips help my siblings the ones that need more help I'm forty-three years old and look at all the stuff I want to be focus on not on gossip and stuff that don't benefit me as a person I'm not worried about if this man has a wife and kids who his messing with to be honest all these years by myself made me realize that I should be focusing not on man, do things to better my life grow as a person and fix my errors and the kids lives that's what I want to focus on for now they do all of this for what I already know the sniffer is the one has him after knowing this don't worry about me I don't want to be part of that anymore in this book I close the chapter this will be the last book you see or hear his name or anything that involves him I needed to put ending that cost me so much harm and pain I had lost so many people that I care about friend and even family members I will never see people the same way

The way this man destroyed my inside, its over thank God also my money finding out the truth which I had been in a life time abuse people doing all type of things and I use to think why? God ,this man did all this for one man all he needed to do was find a way of telling me like he's doing right now even if you not with him I don't want him this man almost destroy my kids lives my life no one is worth all of this he told him that I wrote that piece of paper ever since I had this secret enemy doing all type of harm why he didn't say to me no grace I'm gay whatever I think I would respect you more my error to fall in love with you and show you my feeling I should stay quiet I can change my past but I will change my future how the other guy found out he show him or probably they both laugh about me

It doesn't matter. I learn from this mistakes but you can't blame a thirteen-year-old girl you should say no from the beginning if that was the case, the little ugly ducky wants nothing with you anymore. today is Feb 25 I got up went to the gym pick up my son from the school bus today my day off this people hate me for everything that I do im at the gym and people don't let me work out doing all type of stuff using my own mother against me she's calling me tons of times to record me and staying quiet my mom how can you do that to your daughter, my daughters and I right now we don't have a good relationship how can I joying someone to destroy my daughters life nothing is going to make me betray my own kids I guess everyone think differently fig as my mom as a side a 76-year-old woman you understand how cover was everything

Why so much harm I didn't have a chance of survival he doesn't have a limit I'm writing this book with hope that someone help me with this monster that kills and destroys life and his obsessive to destroy mind his purpose is to limit you in your choices is what he wants never what you want to do for instances if I want to go upstate new york someone is in upstate new york if I want to go new jersey someone is their to that's why I don't care I want to do my own thing and go where I want to go is like holding you hostage I have my rights of going wherever I want they are people that want to create a scenario without you knowing them Sunday morning im at work the fsd gave me a 15 minute break as usual so I went to the Citibank in six avenue and when I go in is man sleeping inside when people go to get money from the ATM that's so wrong people could get rob while you using the machine and I said to the man what you doing I did not show no fear.

But while i'm talking im looking at the ATM and him at the same time his looking out side to see if people are watching and I close the account I had my pepper spray in my pocket and I left quickly. I was a little scared you understand what they do in this book I want to share some the books that I read to help me write this one my journey one of then is start writing your book today, the essential guide getting your book published, this are good books to read and guide you step by step I also went to the library if you want to give a message to the world if you want to share your knowledge or experiences should be the reasons to write a book. That's what they recommend,

On the other hand, is good to have a reflecting to be focus on your inside beauty because the outside years take it right away your inside beauty is forever for instant people use to judge me for not being a regular Dominican girl with long hair my hair is curly a little puffy my hair doesn't define me I could be curly hair my normal weave, clips long ponytail I'm grace in all does different looks and I don't care what others think is people that want to become you they born without an identity like the copy how can you live on what others do or say be your self.changing that topic I truly believe that God is going to restore my finances and triple or much more I still don't get a setup and he still thinks I'm believing him I don't know you It doesn't matter what you say you're a stranger that join the destroy Grace club

A man that in front of me was messing woman and man in all the departments in city college if you decided to become another person to see what you could get from me you are messing wrong fig could do what you were doing mess each other in City College Im going to name the one that i knew ok was doing the girl that after he messes they came back to me he is frustrated with you, of course, you don't have anything just a pussy after he comes his thinking of getting his target was me.specially with people with a lot of envy looking for your destruction if right now I want to go to Jupiter is going to be someone in Jupiter is an strategy that's all out of the same thing that's happening when Im missing ten dollars out my account you understand they want you to leave a mediocre life of misery don't think poor minded is true what I read in a book once, think rich and become rich, misery is not part of me, not Grace, in Gods name I'm escaping from that.

I said this will be the last book that talks about him I really loved him from the first rainy day that he came to the neighborhood

He was tall handsome with his guitar in his hand well dress real slim I like to hear him talk he has this particular voice that calms me down even when he gets little corny I loved everything about this man his smile even if I never be with him I will love you eternity but I have to realize is time to end all this chaos is more man out there that will love me and put me in first place in their life and I had too much to lose for loving him

I want to leave a stress-free life with nobody chasing for my ex is time to close this last chapter and hopefully the psycho sees this and that I'm letting him go forever I also want to say I'm not against gay people you pick and choose who you want to be with im, not God to judge no one I'm against people that want to use woman or man for their convenience to abuse them or take advantage. It's funny but I was singing my destiny when I was five years old the story of my life.

The end

About The Author

Grace E Espiritusanto, the author: I am originally from the Dominican Republic but was raised in New York, and write both non-fictional and semi-fictional novels from the perspective of street smarts. I believes in God. I work in and operate a small book store in Paterson NJ Book fan club im the owner God bless. I hope that reading this non-fiction book will open your (the reader's) eyes.

I'm also the author of the book
My Biggest Sin Loving Hugo My Truths, Fulton Books, May 26, 2020

Made in United States
Troutdale, OR
04/29/2025

30986332R00056